BARNES AND MORTLAKE REMEMBERED

Researched and compiled by members of the Barnes and Mortlake History Society

'Bus Driver: "Barnes Terris! More like 'Wenice in London.'"
BARNES AND THE 'BUS-MAN.
Sketched by a " P.I.P." Artist during the Floods.

Barnes Terrace.   Sketch from the *Penny Illustrated Post* about 1890; by A. J. Finberg, art historian and resident of Barnes.

Front cover: Castelnau, Barnes, 1911 and Owen's, or Adam's, Pond, East Sheen.

Published by Hendon Publishing Co., Ltd., Hendon Mill, Nelson, Lancashire.
Text © Barnes and Mortlake History Society, 1988.
Printed by Fretwell & Cox Ltd., Goulbourne Street, Keighley, West Yorkshire, BD21 1PZ.

Introduction

Some ten years ago the Barnes and Mortlake History Society produced *Barnes and Mortlake As It Was* and *Vintage Barnes and Mortlake* in collaboration with Hendon Publishing Company. The demand for them has since resulted in a number of reprints and we have decided to supplement them with a further collection. There is no lack of material as interesting early photographs continue to come to light and others acquire 'vintage status' through the passing of time. For space reasons certain houses and places were omitted before, as also from *Glimpses of Old Barnes and Mortlake,* our miscellany of prints and drawings of the district. Our new collection has become *Barnes and Mortlake Remembered.*

Over the past decade there have been many further changes to the local scene, and, in particular, the smaller older buildings tend to disappear or be subjected to drastic alteration. Barnes has perhaps altered less than its neighbours but now has a rebuilt parish church in a vigorous contemporary style. On a more mundane level, the uninspiring 1938 'Bull' at East Sheen has been demolished and replaced by an even drearier shopping parade after less than fifty years. The process will, of course, continue, and it is fascinating to compare how our area looks today with the aerial photographs taken between the wars.

Our approach to local history has also subtlely changed and we hope that this too is reflected in our selection. We are naturally restricted by what the photographers chose as their subjects and what has survived. In particular, the older photographs are necessarily more static and contrived but after the turn of the century far greater spontaneity was possible. Nearly all the illustrations are worth the closest scrutiny for minor details of local history, and, quite frequently, the local residents take over as the main subjects, rehearsing a concert or a play, or watching an almost forgotten happening such as the Mortlake Missionary Convention Parade or a fashionable balloon race at Ranelagh.

Barnes and Mortlake Remembered follows the same format as its predecessors, a logical visual tour with the help of a map pin-pointing the locations of all the illustrations. It is, of course, restricted to the areas contained in the old parishes of Barnes and Mortlake including East Sheen and a sizeable chunk of Richmond Park. We hope that it will give as much pleasure as it companion volumes.

Richard Jeffree

BARNES

1. Mill Lodge, 1904. Originally the site was Mill Farm and records go back well into the eighteenth century, but by the mid-nineteenth century alterations and enlargements had taken place. Around 1880 the house became the family home of Mr Samuel Keene JP, his wife and innumerable children. After the deaths of Mr and Mrs Keene, soon after the turn of the century, the house was used by Harrods as a club-house for their extensive sports-ground, which is still open land.

2. Holy Trinity Church, Castelnau. This photograph of Holy Trinity Church shows the interior prior to the extension of the chancel in 1913; then the only door into the vestry was on the left side of the sanctuary and the gas lamps were much in evidence. The east window was shattered by a bomb in the Second World War and has been replaced by one of different design. The pews are still in use today although the original doors and the tops at each end have been removed.

3. Castelnau, 1911. Posted from 89 Castelnau on 8 May 1911 this card says: 'Got here in time for tea. They were having it late after the Albert Hall concert. Love E.T.' An open-topped solid-tyred motor bus can be seen; six De Dions were introduced at Mortlake garage in 1906. The bend in Castelnau seen here is due to a fortunate change in the plans of the Hammersmith Bridge Company which made the road in 1827. The proposed route would have gone straight through Barnes Pond, but of this only the north-eastern portion in line with the bridge was retained, the remainder being diverted as of now across Barnes Common. It was first called Upper Bridge Road.

4. The Lobjoit family group. Members of the Lobjoit family enjoy a summer's day in the cottage garden at Barn Elms Farm. The farm was once the Home Farm of the Manorial estate. The Lobjoits were large-scale market gardeners in Surrey and Middlesex. They were in Barnes from 1832 until 1895, where they raised Lobjoit's English Cos Lettuce. William and Edward Lobjoit were the last occupants of Barn Elms Farm from 1893 until 1895, when it was bought by the West Middlesex Water Company. In March 1897, farmhouse, cottage and land were all drowned beneath the Company's reservoirs.

A BALLOON RACE FROM RANELAGH.—MR. FRANK H. BUTLER'S DOLCE FAR NIENTE, WINNER, FOLLOWING MR. C. F. POLLOCK'S AERO CLUB III. (SECOND).

In this race, which took place last Saturday, the prize went to the balloon which alighted nearest to Ingatestone, in Essex. Mr. Butler's balloon, which won the first prize, carried Col. and Mrs. Capper, while Aero Club III's passengers included Princess di Teano and Viscount Royston.

5. **Balloons at Ranelagh.** Apart from polo and other sporting and social activities the club played an important part in the early development of flying. The Royal Aero Club was founded in the basket of a balloon in 1901, and the first flying meeting was held in the following year at Ranelagh, which continued to be the club's main base till 1908. This picture is from a periodical of 1907 which describes balloon racing as 'the latest society craze'. The Ranelagh Club polo pavilion is seen in the background.

6. **Drama scene.** A tense moment from J.B. Priestley's *Dangerous Corner* as presented by Gladys Rees's Riverside Repertory Company at St Mary's Church Hall, Kitson Road, *c.* 1937; included here are Frank Jeffree (second from left), Marjorie Hayward (girl in white) and Enid Chambers (extreme right). The young man in the centre is Tony Clayden, still a popular local resident.

Front of Convent of the Sacred Heart, 45, Church Road, Barnes, S. W.

7. **The Convent of the Sacred Heart, Church Road.** The Sisters of the Order of the Sacred Hart came to Barnes at the turn of the century with the intention of running a nursing home. Before their plans were complete several parents asked if they would give their daughters private French lessons. A small group of girls met in a greenhouse in the garden and when the news of this class spread more requests came in. The Sisters realised the local demand was for a school not a nursing home, and consequently set about to supply this need. The number of pupils increased so rapidly that a large school building of two stories was erected on the former orchard. Boys were admitted up to the age of eight, and a number of French girls came over as boarders in order to learn English. The one-storey building on the left of The Lawn, as the house had formerly been named, was the chapel. The Sisters left Barnes in the 1970s, and the school is now St Osmund's Primary School.

8. Church Road looking east, c. 1920. This view has changed little during the last sixty years. There is no longer a shop between the Sun Inn and the Bank building, and the open-topped bus would hardly be acceptable today to those travelling to town in all weathers. The frequency of the No. 9 service every three or four minutes was taken for granted then and request signs were not necessary as a bus pulled up for a passenger anywhere along the route when signalled to by a raised arm.

9. Aerial view of Barnes Pond, 1920. The sheet of water in the centre of this illustration shows Barnes Pond with the Green School, now the Day Centre, on the east side. The shape of the Crescent can easily be identified, and it is interesting to note the large gardens of both Essex and Milbourne Houses. These gardens stretched down to Stanton Road and are now covered by Essex Court. The buildings to the left of the Methodist Church were Cleveland Cottage and Cleveland House. The tall building at the corner of Stanton and Cleveland roads had been originally intended as an hotel. This venture proved a failure and soon after Canon Kitson became rector the premises were used by the parish as a Church Hall. By the time this photograph was taken it was occupied by a Limited Company manufacturing St Jacob's Oil.

10.   Essex House, Barnes Green.   Here, on a summer's day *c.* 1910, Maud Hamilton, aged fourteen, is playing croquet with her friends. The house was the residence of Dr Hamilton, who had a local practice and drove round in a pony and trap to visit his patients. The croquet lawn was divided by two large trees from a tennis court, and beyond that a high wall separated the grounds from Stanton Road.

11.   Cleveland House, Barnes Green, *c.* 1885.   The Wilkinson family are standing at the garden entrance to their house overlooking Barnes Green. Built about 1705 it commanded an excellent view of the pond, while what is now Station Road passed the front door. The house had many uses before its demolition in the 1930s: besides being a private residence it had served as a boys' boarding school from 1821 to 1860, and after the Wilkinson's day it became a laundry and in the 1920s, after many alterations, it was a chocolate, cake and ice-cream factory. It now serves as a postal sorting office and the Admiralty patent office.

12.   Barnes Methodist Church, Station Road; the opening ceremony, Wednesday, 19 September 1906.   The congregation braves the rain to pose for the photographer, the ladies looking worried about their splendid hats. The Methodists arrived in Barnes *c.* 1860, as visitors to the gipsy encampment behind the cemetery on Barnes Common. Shortly after, regular open-air meetings were held on Barnes Green. A small chapel, built in White Hart Lane in 1867, was soon outgrown — it survives as the Barnes Church and Healing Centre. The new large Wesleyan Church, built on the grounds of Cleveland House, cost £6,000. The first service was on Sunday, 23 September 1906, when a baptism was performed by the Reverend Joseph Olphert.

13. Beverley Brook, Barnes. The footbridge across the brook marks the dividing line between the Green and the Common — or the Waste as it was called in eighteenth-century Vestry Minutes. This photograph, taken at the turn of the century, shows clearly the three houses which still stand in Station Road facing open ground. The garden fence of Cleveland Cottage and House, which occupied the land on which the Methodist Church and its ancillary buildings were erected, can be easily identified.

14. The approach to Barnes Station, Barnes Common; the 'rush hour', 1911. Bowler-hatted city gents step out smartly to catch the morning train to town. Present day commuters will doubtless recognise the scene, the difference being the small number of travellers compared with today, and the absence of cars parked at the kerb-side. And, of course, commuting to the city is no longer a male prerogative. Glimpsed through the trees is the quaint mock-Tudor station building, *c.* 1846, which never fails to surprise one by its very presence in the midst of a rural setting.

15. Barnes Cemetery, Barnes Common, 1916.
Founded in 1854 on two acres of common purchased by the church authorities from the Lords of the Manor for £10, it is no longer in use. Several distinguished Victorians lie buried there alongside the more ordinary folk of Barnes. Its neat appearance, pictured here, contrasts sharply with its present state of neglect. The lodge and railings went shortly after the Borough Council took control in 1966, since when almost every tombstone has been vandalised. Nature has concealed the worst of the damage beneath a luxuriant carpet of wild flowers, and its sad beauty attracts walkers to the spot despite stories of murder and ghosts long associated with the place. In recent years it has been featured in several 'horror movies'.

16. Barnes High Street looking west. Shopping was a leisurely business before the First World War and there was many a quiet gossip in the High Street. The telegraph boys wait around the Post Office door ready to cycle off when there is a telegram to deliver. The errand boy has left the trolley outside Best's wine shop so that he can wheel home a crate of goods for a customer. The wall on the extreme right was that of Threlkeld House, the site now is that of Seaforth Lodge.

17.   Barnes High Street looking west, *c.* 1910.   Lilley and Skinner's shoe shop, on the corner of St Ann's Road, displays the fashionable footwear of the period. It closed down at the end of the 1920s. Opposite was the fishmonger and poulterer, Mr Bailey, who also had a second shop in Church Road looking on to The Crescent. The children standing in the street in their neat caps and suits add much to the local scene.

18. Barnes High Street looking east.   This view of the river end of the High Street, looking towards the Sun Inn, shows the cottages which formerly stood on the site of the present police garage. The lamp jutting out from the front of the house opposite the Coach and Horses was to show the residence of Mr Vine, the sweep. Here orders could be left to book his services, which were much in demand by housewives at spring-cleaning time. The absence of pedestrians and traffic is in marked contrast to the bustle of today.

19. Reuben Bell's butcher's shop.   This shop stood at 66 Railway Street (now Westfields Avenue) and was kept by a well-beloved local personality. He delivered the meat himself on a butcher's tray and his pet lamb and goose followed behind. Even when too old to work he dressed daily in his butcher's outfit and, thus arrayed, sat down to read the paper. He died in September 1931, aged ninety.

20.   **Westfields School, Archway Street.**   This group of children were pupils at Westfields Infant and Junior School in 1930. The school had been opened with 170 pupils in 1903 as the population in that area had increased considerably and the former building, on an opposite site, could no longer house both senior girls and the younger children. The original entrance was in Railway Street, now Westfields Avenue.

MORTLAKE

21. & 22.   Marsham Lodge.   This house, the first in Mortlake, was separated by a passageway from the White Hart in Barnes. Despite alterations over the centuries it could still be identified as an Elizabethan structure with some Tudor panelling, a large coat of arms of Protector Seymour, Duke of Somerset, and an elegant early eighteenth-century fireplace. The interior view shows the house furnished in the time of Dr R. D. Macintosh, who lived here for nearly forty years until its demolition by the local authority in 1930.

23. Council Depot, Mortlake. The staff pose for the camera on the opening day — workmen in their Sunday best, polished horse brasses and harness, and the necessity to keep perfectly still for such a wide photograph. Barnes Urban District Council acquired The Limes, Mortlake High Street, in 1895 and held its first meeting there in November that year. The purchase price of £4,000 (together with alterations) included the lands attached to the house. The electricity works were built on the western part and the Council Depot and Yard laid out on the eastern side, the stables being erected about 1897. The whole complex now forms Tide Way Yard.

24.   Castelnau House.   This house faced the end of Ashleigh Road, which was constructed over its grounds. The Boileau family lived here for over a century and named it Castelnau Place after their ancestral home in France. They rebuilt the part overlooking the river. In 1894 it became a girls' school known as Ashleigh College. It was demolished by the local authority in 1907. The staircase, dating from about 1680, is preserved at the Victoria and Albert Museum.

25. Mortlake Parish Church.   The screen enclosing the Lady Chapel was erected in 1936 as a memorial, but was swept away in the re-ordering of the church effected in 1982. The wall monument is the church's greatest artistic treasure. It commemorates Francis Coventry, who died in 1699. It has the signature of the sculptor William Kidwell, and is considered to be his finest work. Pevsner describes it as a fine rich luxuriant piece.

26. Mortlake Parish Church Vestry.   In 1794 Benjamin Vandergucht, artist and picture dealer, presented to the church a painting of the *Entombment of Christ* by Gerhard Seghers. Modern scholarship attributes it to the studio of Rubens. This originally formed a reredos at the east end but was subsequently relegated to the Vestry where it remained until 1980 and has since been sold. At the foot of the picture can be seen the coat of arms of the donor, who lost his life while crossing the river from Chiswick shortly after his gift. *(By permission of the Royal Commission on the Historical Monuments of England).*

MORTLAKE
PAROCHIAL SCHOOLS.
SUPPORTED BY VOLUNTARY
CONTRIBUTIONS.

FOUNDED A.D. 1700.

PARTLY ENDOWED A.D. 1719.

ENLARGED A.D. 1815.
RECONSTRUCTED A.D. 1894.

27. Burton's tomb. The celebrated tomb in the form of a tent in St Mary Magdalen's R.C. churchyard, South Worple Way, Mortlake, which contains the remains of Sir Richard Francis Burton (1821–1890) explorer, diplomat and scholar, and his wife Isabel. He was received into the Roman Catholic faith on the point of death. There is a small altar, and the gilt coffins are set with coloured glass. On opening the massive stone door camel bells would ring, but in 1951 it was forced, presumably for the fabled but mythological gold and precious stones within. The door was then bricked up. Since then there has been extensive restoration. A ladder at the back permits a view of the interior. On 22 January every year a Mass of Repose is said for the souls of the occupants.

28. Tablet. The Mortlake Workhouse or Poorhouse faced Vineyard Path at the corner of Mullins Path. Approached through Workhouse Path between the present Rann House and Craven House flats, the workhouse closed when in 1836 the inmates moved to the Richmond Union. This tablet formerly on the north wall records the first conversion of the building into schools in 1894, becoming part of St Mary's Church of England Schools which closed in 1982. The workhouse, now converted into Capel Court (named for the Lady Capel, died 1721, benefactress to Mortlake charity schools), has been given back its pitched roof and restored very approximately to its original appearance.

29. Mortlake High Street, 1905.   High Street seen from near the Green on a postcard dated 2 August 1905. The last buildings were pulled down in 1971 for road widening. Proceeding left is Wrights (butcher and slaughter house), old Vineyard Path entry, off-licence, and baker. The extended shop front is the Sheen Invicta Sanitary Laundry (later Wainwright & Waring). The postcard sender has marked with a cross 'my schoolroom windows' above the shop. Next is the Trots Alley entrance. Further along projects the sign of The Hope beerhouse (later dining rooms and Platts Stores, containing post office). The cone of the malthouse kiln went after the last war.

30. Cottages in Littleworth End. When a Victorian photographer appeared with plate camera and black velvet cloth a few curious but cautious onlookers were attracted, as in this study of four cottages on the south side of the Lower Richmond Road, west of the Jolly Milkman in Littleworth End, Mortlake. Projecting beyond the cottages, with their necessary security shutters and pleasing gothicisms in the window glazing, is West End House which still stands. From this point the road became a quiet lane leading through fields and market gardens to Richmond.

31. Littleworth End shop. An atmospheric afternoon in Littleworth End, west of Mortlake Green. Its unromantic alias was West End. The Lower Richmond Road passes by with evidence of horse traffic. A signwriter's fist points the way to The Ship at the bottom of Ship Lane which is opposite. The little shop displays advertisements for Eiffel Tower Lemonade, Liptons Tea and Rowntrees Cocoa. The Jolly Milkman lays well back behind the third house. It provided, as the sign says, Accommodation for Commmercials and Cyclists, and hot dinners from midday until two o'clock. Sixpence bought two veg and a choice of beef steak pudding or a cut from the joint.

32. The Ship Inn, Mortlake. The Ship Inn on Thames Bank, Mortlake, seen here with a large gasolier lighting the entrance, goes back at least four centuries. It was then variously The Harts Horn or The Hartshorns, with custom from the nearby drawdock, the 'wharfe' in Elizabethan times, with a tradition of an underwater causeway to the Chiswick shore. In the early 1600s it was The Blue Anchor. Shortened to The Anchor it had a companion in The Maidenhead at the corner of Princes Court (Aynscombe Path). Charles John Phillips, the Mortlake brewer, in the 1850s acquired the Ship Alehouse 'with the Long Room in front divided into four rooms' and an adjoining boathouse. The pub was subsequently rebuilt.

33. Leyden House, Thames Bank. An early photograph of the garden front dating from the 1850s. It depicts the west wing, in which over sixty years ago an early Tudor fireplace was discovered. The bow was added in the eighteenth century. In 1845 the house was taken by Sir Henry Taylor, a dramatic poet well known in his day. He called it Ladon House since the lines 'Nymphs and shepherds trip no more by sandy Ladon's lilied banks' were in his head when he went to see it.

34.   The Harding-Sullivan sculling match from Putney to Mortlake, 1895.   The local river scene is the setting for many important events in the rowing calendar. The match shown here took place on 9 September 1895 from Putney to Mortlake. It was for the Sculling Championship of England and £400, a very large sum at the time. The contenders, Tom Sullivan of Hammersmith, who stood 6ft. 1in. and weighed 12st., and C.R. Harding of Chelsea, who was 5ft. 5in. and weighed 9st. 5lb., are seen after the finish, surrounded by eights and numerous small craft. Spectators line the Mortlake river bank and the deck of the steamer to cheer the winner, C.R. Harding. In the background is the Mortlake Brewery, showing the fine chimney demolished in December 1975.

35. Chiswick Bridge.   Chiswick Bridge, Sir Herbert Baker's masterpiece, nears completion. The name Mortlake Bridge was suggested, but the *Barnes & Mortlake Herald* thought it was 'not likely to be of any use to the inhabitants'. The Chiswick approach road was built in 1923 to alleviate unemployment. Seven years later the Cleveland Bridge Co. won the £208,284 contract. Building took two years with 175–200 workmen and (in tons) 45,000 concrete, 6,000 cement, 3,400 Portland stone and 750 steel reinforcement. The steam tug was constantly on safety patrol. The bridge was opened by the then Prince of Wales (a native of Mortlake), who whisked past ranks of schoolchildren on Monday, 3 July 1933 to cut the ribbon with scissors designed by Sir Edwin Lutyens. The second Cromwell House, near the bridge on Thames Bank, was demolished 1947. The entrance to Cubbit's Yacht Basin is top left.

36. Cromwell House. Old Cromwell House faced the Lower Richmond Road and its grounds extended northwards to the Thames. It may have derived its name from Thomas Cromwell who was Lord of the Manor, and whose brother-in-law had a brewery in Mortlake. After being occupied by Edward Colston, the great Bristol philanthropist, it was long unoccupied and was demolished in 1858. The entrance gate seen in the photograph remained *in situ* until 1962 when it was moved a short distance to the west. The site is now covered by industrial premises.

37. Phillips & Wigan trade card. The trade card of Phillips & Wigan, the Mortlake brewers. Charles John Phillips, aged twenty-six, took over the concern, then called the Star Brewery, in 1846. He went into partnership with James Wigan in 1852. The P&W monogram adorns the High Street façade each side of the *Mortlake Brewery 1869* inscription. The partnership was dissolved by 1877. Phillips took two sons into the firm as Phillips & Co., combining with Watney & Co. in 1889. Further brewery amalgamations formed Watney, Combe, Reid & Co. The title of Stag Brewery was assumed in 1982. The actual size of the card is a most impressive 5·7in. × 8·7in.

EAST SHEEN

38. Sheen Vale Orchestra. During the 1920s and 1930s there were numerous local groups of amateur performing companies in the area. Here the Sheen Vale Orchestral Society are giving an outdoor concert during their summer season, transporting not only their personal instruments but also a harmonium. The announcement of the bi-weekly rehearsals says much for their enthusiasm.

39. Portobello House.   Vice Admiral Mayne took part in the battle of Portobello under Admiral Vernon, and on his retirement in 1747 he built this house in Worple Way on the edge of the village. Flags and cannon were carved in the pediment on the entrance front. The house was demolished in 1893. Its site was near the north end of Howgate Road.

40.   The Mortlake Convention.   It is shortly after 4.45 p.m. on Thursday, 18 June 1914, the second day of the three-day Diocesan Missionary Convention, an outstanding event in Mortlake church history. Shoppers pause to stare, and boys in celluloid collars gaze in wonder as church dignitaries, led by the vicar of Mortlake, the Reverend Horace Monroe, process down Sheen Lane, followed by a large crowd. The procession is *en route* to the Parish Church, following a meeting held in a giant marquee in the grounds of The Cedars, East Sheen, at which more than 1,400 people were present and where over 800 teas were served by the parish ladies in less than a quarter of an hour! Speakers at the convention included the Bishops of Southwark, London and Kingston. The final events were a garden party at East Sheen Lodge, marred by a heavy thunderstorm, followed by a service at Southwark Cathedral.

41. The Bull Inn. The Bull Inn, East Sheen, seen here, was built in 1792 by Mr J. C. Halford, the then owner of Mortlake Brewery, on the site of an earlier seventeenth-century inn. It was the stopping place on several coach routes, where the horses were changed and stabled in the yard at the rear. It was rebuilt in 1938 as the Bull Hotel and Penrhyn Rooms, which were demolished in 1987.

42. The Triangle, East Sheen. Milestone Green, alias The Triangle, East Sheen, in the late 1920s. The quaint Picturedrome cinema opened on Boxing Day 1911 with seats at 3*d.*, 6*d.*, and one shilling, with free afternoon teas except for the threepennies. In this view the attraction is *Thelma* starring Jane Novak. The cinema was replaced by the Sheen Kinema (later The Empire) in 1930. It closed in 1961 and Parkway House was built on the site. The war memorial of Cornish granite was unveiled in April 1925. A glass cylinder containing the names of 249 of the fallen was buried beneath the Sword of Sacrifice. Amongst discarded ideas for the memorial was a clocktower with the names inscribed on its sides.

43. **Upper Richmond Road looking east.** When the Leycester-Penrhyn family left The Cedars, Sheen Lane, in 1919 they presented land for road widening where hitherto a high wall had stood. This is recorded in an inscription in the pavement, in the foreground, near the corner of Sheen Gate Gardens from where this photograph was taken. The next owner erected advertisement hoardings along the new boundary, which remained until the present parade of shops was built in 1931.

44. Ivy House, East Sheen. Ivy House was opposite Milestone Green (The Triangle). Here lived John Sanders (died 1841), second owner of the pottery on the Mortlake waterside east of Bulls Alley, and then, lastly, a Madame Feste. The house was replaced *c.* 1899 by Rosa Pavement, the four shops at 246–252 Upper Richmond Road. No. 250 for many years housed the East Sheen post office in Medus's (now a newsagent's shop). There is a glimpse of the white house of William Dunkley, butcher and grazier, at the corner of Sheen Lane. John Perring went into the building which took its place, hence Perring's Corner.

45. Milestone Green. This photograph, looking down Sheen Lane, was taken about 1905. On the right can be seen the end of the row of shops recently built on the site of Ivy House. The house of William Dunkley still stood on the corner, soon to be replaced by what was long known as Perring's corner. Colston's Almshouses are on the left, and in the distance are the newly-built shops on the corner of St Leonard's Road.

46.   Sheen House cycing track.   Sheen House Cycling Club Ltd., registered in 1896, constructed the track in cement upon an embankment within the twenty-acre estate of Sheen House. There were four laps to the mile, and bicycle polo was played within the 100-yard diameter circle. Sheen Lane is marked by the line of trees behind the house, to the right of which Shrewsbury Avenue now passes. Sheen House was demolished in 1907, and Shrewsbury Avenue and Muirdown Avenue were developed on the site of the northern half of the track in 1923. The path of the former track crosses Richmond Park Road at, approximately, Nos. 37 and 32 and Shrewsbury Avenue at Nos. 8 and 11, continuing in the grounds of Barnes Home Guard Association. Berwick Avenue, to run south of and parallel with Shrewsbury Avenue, was never built.

47.   The Firs, Sheen Lane.   Throughout the eighteenth century this house belonged to the Godschall family, Dutch merchants in the City. In the 1840s it was owned by George Twining, tea merchant and banker. About 1902 Sheen Gate Gardens and Firs Avenue were laid out over its grounds but the house survived until about 1947, when it was demolished as a result of enemy action. Nos. 190 and 192 Sheen Lane stand on the site.

48. East Sheen Lodge.   The Earl of Fife acquired the house in 1880. In 1889 he married Princess Louise, eldest daughter of the Prince and Princess of Wales, and was elevated to a dukedom. This photograph, from an album of Princess Victoria, the Duchess' sister, dates from 1890 and shows the Duke and Duchess standing on the terrace outside the Reception Hall. They continued to live here until 1905. The house was demolished in 1965. Nos. 59 to 71 York Avenue stand on the site.
(Copyright reserved. Reproduced by gracious permission of Her Majesty The Queen).

49. East Sheen Avenue.   The approach to Palewell Common from East Sheen was for centuries by way of a lane from Milestone Green. Park Avenue marks the site of part of it. In 1807, following action taken by Henry Hope of Sheen House, the first section was closed and the alternative route provided is now East Sheen Avenue. This photograph was taken when the elms which Hope planted were still flourishing.

50. Palewell Pond. Constructed in the 1920s near the site of the Pale Well, the pond on Palewell Common was originally a natural pond prone to flooding and land drainage problems. It was a favourite venue for the sailing of boats and for paddling. The surrounding trees grew over the years to their full height only to be destroyed in the storms of October 1987.

51. Boating pool. Owen's Pond, alias Adam's Pond, near the East Sheen Gate of Richmond Park served as a boating pool in the summers between Easter 1930 and the outbreak of the war in September 1939. Boys of a mechanical disposition favoured the paddlewheelers, but it was thought more adventurous to go in a canoe or rowboat. Tickets were bought at the shed on a time basis and when this expired the boat was called in ('Come in number two!'). Some boys would show off by ignoring the summons until they were hauled ashore by the attendant with his long boat-hook. Few could afford the trifling pence for a second trip on the same visit. The landing stage remains, but Sheen Cottage against the park wall was destroyed by enemy action in the last war. Here lived Professor Sir Richard Owen, the naturalist, between 1852 and 1892. The alternative name for the pond came from William Adam who resided there between 1787 and 1816. The pond is in Mortlake.

52. An aerial view of East Sheen.   This aerial view of part of Sheen adjacent to Sheen Gate was taken in 1936. Note the almost total absence of cars. It shows East Sheen Lodge (centre background) and the curves of Richmond Park Road and Palewell Park. Of particular note is the Chinese teahouse in the grounds of Sheen Lawn Tennis Club (left of centre foreground) which had been transported on rollers from the garden of East Sheen Lodge in 1926 only to be destroyed by fire in 1973.

53. & 54.   Parkholme, Fife Road.   This house was built about 1876 adjoining Richmond Park and Sheen Common. Until 1890 Fife Road came to an end at this point. Its most distinguished occupant was the actor-manager Sir John Martin-Harvey who was here for fifteen years until 1938. The bust standing in the entrance hall is of Sir Henry Irving. With it stood a bust by Frampton of Martin-Harvey in his most famous role as Sydney Carton in *The Only Way*. After the war the house was converted into two dwellings, Nos. 28 and 30 Fife Road.

55. Sheen Lane. This view from the corner of Fife Road was taken in 1924, shortly before building development began on both sides. On the left a high wall ran down almost to Christ Church Road, broken only by the imposing entrance gates of East Sheen Lodge. On the right, as far as Stonehill Road, was an open fence backed by a hedge through which were glimpses of the massive pile of Clare Lawn rising beyond the parkland.

56. Sheen Common pavilion. This original pavilion stood at the far end of the Common adjoining the Park wall. Teas and light refreshments could be obtained during the summer months, and a full time Common keeper took bookings for the tennis courts which he kept an eye on from his office. He also overlooked the care of the flower beds, bowling green and sports pitches.

57. East Sheen Common. In 1859 Earl Spencer as Lord of the Manor gave permission to local Volunteers to set up a rifle range, and this continued until 1880 when the neighbouring residents purchased the manorial rights to enable them to terminate the practice. This photograph taken in 1893 shows the remains of the stop-butt with the trees of Richmond Park behind, after a gale had blown down six of the seven supporting buttresses.

58. Sheen Wood. The cottage shown here stood in Christ Church Road, west of Percy Lodge. It was purchased in the 1860s as a country cottage by Frederick Walford, who is seen in the picture with two grandchildren. Later he pulled it down and built a house which he called Ste Croix, but was subsequently renamed Sheen Wood. This house was in turn demolished in 1937.

59. Martindale. This road was constructed about 1910 over the grounds of Spencer House which stood on the site of Spencer Gardens and was demolished about 1907. It has been owned by the Reeves family for over a century.
The belt of trees beyond formed part of the Temple Grove estate and disappeared to make way for Percival Road a few years later.

60. The Planes, Temple Sheen, showing the south front from Christ Church Road. There was a house here in the seventeenth century. At one period it was called Chain Hall. Sir Francis Ommanney, a leading figure in Mortlake for many years, lived here, succeeding the Browne family. He died in 1840. His sons followed and made many alterations. Its name derived from two very large plane trees near the stable block (now Mullion Cottage, Well Lane). The house was demolished in 1935. The gateway in the foreground still stands.

61. The Bailiff's House, King's Farm. The Bailiff's House photographed shortly before its demolition in 1899. The 80-acre farm was within the old parish of Mortlake, east of present-day Manor Road. It was purchased by Queen Caroline in 1746 and later belonged to 'farmer' George III, hence the name it came to be known by. From the nineteenth until the early part of the present century, the remaining open land was used as a market garden, some of which survives as allotments bordering the railway at North Sheen. The farm is commemorated by King's Farm Avenue, laid out on part of the site in 1928.

62. Derby Stores, Derby Road. In 1907 Mr F.H. Hewett obtained a licence to sell the products of Mortlake Brewery at his general stores in Derby Road. Here, he and his wife are standing in the doorway of their shop from which customers could also buy stamps and leave parcels for the London carriers, Carter Paterson & Co. Two years later the Hewetts moved to the Victoria Inn and George Hewett, a relative, took over the business. After a number of different owners the shop closed in the 1970s and is now a private residence. The wisteria is still a feature and grows across the front of six cottages.